ZOUAVES

The First and The Bravest.

by
Michael J. McAfee

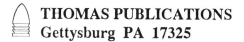
THOMAS PUBLICATIONS
Gettysburg PA 17325

Copyright © 1991 Michael J. McAfee

Printed and bound in the United States of America

Published by THOMAS PUBLICATIONS, Gettysburg, Pa. 17325

All rights reserved. No part of this book may be used or reproduced without written permission of the author and the publisher, except in the case of brief quotations embodied in critical essays and reviews.

ISBN-0-939631-37-7

Front cover painting by Don Troiani courtesy of Historical Art Prints, Ltd., P.O. Box 660, Southbury, CT 06488.

Front cover design by Ryan C. Stouch.

CONTENTS

PREFACE 5

INTRODUCTION 7

LES ZOUAVES 9

CRIMEA AND ITALY 14

THE ZOUAVE UNIFORM 20

ELMER E. ELLSWORTH AND THE AMERICAN ZOUAVE 25

ZOUAVES OF THE CIVIL WAR 39

UNIFORMS OF THE CIVIL WAR ZOUAVE 90

NOTES 117

BIBLIOGRAPHY 119

INDEX 120

PREFACE

In 1979, the West Point Museum, at the United States Military Academy, West Point, New York, opened a temporary exhibit entitled "Zouaves...the First and the Bravest." This exhibition drew upon the extensive artifacts collections of the museum, and was the first such exhibit of zouave memorabilia.

At that time the author prepared a brief account of the history of the zouave in the nineteenth century which was published as an exhibit catalogue. It proved to be so popular that it went through three publishings. Now, in conjunction with Mr. Dean Thomas, this second account of the zouave and his legend is published. The original text has been revised and slightly enlarged, but more importantly, new and better illustrations have been added to the original concept.

The story of the zouave is practically lost to history. Certainly the American public knows nothing of him, and even Civil War enthusiasts often have a distorted view of his role in the Civil War. Obviously zouaves did not win the American Civil War. They did, however, contribute more than just color to that conflict. With that in mind we offer the reader this brief account of "the First and the Bravest."

Michael J. McAfee
Newburgh, New York

INTRODUCTION

Warfare in the nineteenth century was no less bloody than today, yet people of the Victorian era saw it as a romantic adventure. Their vision of the battlefield was largely formed by the art of the period. Normally, early nineteenth century military art was limited to depictions of immense fields of battle, miraculously devoid of smoke and confusion, with any action centering around a prominent general on horseback. The most common of military art, created for the masses, consisted of cheap lithographs, crudely drawn and even though filled with blood and gore, curiously unrealistic. As a result, the Victorian mind was able to view war through a veil of romanticism and hide from sight those aspects it preferred not to see. As warfare was then associated with glory, patriotism and heroism, it was only natural that the warrior should share in those virtues. The wretched, often brutal, life of the common soldier was ignored as was his lowly status in society. Only the most visible, colorful or romantic of soldiers were allowed to intrude upon society in the Victorian age. In England, the proud Guards regiments and romantic Highlanders were the chosen representatives of the British soldier. They were the ideal types. In France it was the Chasseurs and the Zouaves who received similar public notice. They became the stereotypes for bravery and to a degree their own lives as soldiers were enhanced by this attention.

None were more heroic in lithographs or paintings than the Zouave. He seemed the "beau-ideal of a soldier," as General George B. McClellan, of Civil War fame, described him. The French Zouaves enjoyed a reputation of being recklessly brave on the battlefield, as though warfare was merely a game and their lives simply the table stakes.

Their conduct off the battlefield was equally notable, for they tended to be undisciplined, resourceful foragers who provided for their personal comfort in any manner which was practical and the "liberation" of goods meant little to men who could expect to die in their next combat. Yet, they were not brigands. They were members of an elite unit with an *esprit de corps* which bound them together as a family, with the regimental commander, known as "Father" among the Zouaves, as the family head. They were also bound together by their distinctive dress. The Arab-inspired short jacket, baggy trousers and fez were key parts of their identity.

The Zouave became a Victorian ideal of a soldier. He was not afraid to die in combat for he looked upon battle as a field of honor. Yet, he was human and capable of emotion, whether rage on the battlefield or deep sorrow at the death of a comrade.

The end of the Victorian era — and it died in the muddy Flanders fields in 1914 with thousands of brave soldiers — also meant the end of the Zouave. He was a product of Victorian sentimentality and could not survive the twentieth century in the same form. The French Army retains units of Zouaves, but they no longer wear distinctive uniforms. In America zouaves lasted into the 1950s in the form of an American Legion drill team, even appearing on the Ed Sullivan Show in their twilight years. But the true Zouave, the gallant rascal of the nineteenth century, is gone forever.

* * *

LES ZOUAVES

The Zouaves of the French Army were originally recruited from native North African troops. Early in 1830 France launched an expedition into Algeria and in July of that year the city of Algiers was captured by a French Army. In August a number of Algerians (mainly Kabyles [Berbers]) of the Zouaoua tribe offered their services to the occupying army. The French general staff, feeling they could be useful in maintaining order and protecting the city accepted them, and on 1 October they were organized into two battalions under French officers. A few French volunteers joined the native contingent at that time, setting the precedent for further European enlistments. It was not until March of 1831, however, that these troops were officially sanctioned by King Louis Philippe. By 1835 the Zouave corps consisted of two battalions of six companies (two of French and four of Arabs), which could be increased in size to ten companies.[1]

Rapidly, however, more and more Frenchmen were brought into the Zouave battalions. One officer described the process in his reminiscences:

> The uniform — the manner of life — the greater liberty there enjoyed, than in the garrisons of France, or even of Algeria, — the certainty of being present wherever a musket shot was to be fired, — the glory to be acquired, — were, all of them, considerations well calculated to attract into our ranks the descendants of those Gauls, our forefathers; whose proud saying it was that, *"WERE THE HEAVENS THEMSELVES TO FALL, THEY WOULD YET BEAR THEM UP ON THE STEEL OF THEIR LANCES."*[2]

By 1841, when the Zouaves were reorganized into three battalions, only one company of nine was formed from native soldiers. Gradually, all North Africans were put into independent battalions of sharpshooters until the Zouave companies were all European. In 1852, three regiments of Zouaves were authorized, with each of the three original battalions serving as the nucleus of a new regiment. Each regiment had a provincial headquarters: Blidah, for the 1st; Oran for the 2nd; and Constantine for the 3rd.[3] Filling these regiments presented no problem, for there were many veteran soldiers in North Africa "eager to be allowed to wear a uniform already illustrated by feats of arms, which...had already won for the corps an imperishable renown for bravery."[4] The skill of the Zouave battalions as light infantry and skirmishes had made them invaluable during the conquest of North Africa. They rapidly developed an *esprit de corps* which put them apart from other soldiers:

> They are proud of their uniform, which resembles that of no other corps; proud of their name, of an origin so singular and mysterious; proud of the daring act of gallantry, with which they are constantly enriching the history of their corps; and happy in the freedom which is permitted them, whether in garrison or on the march.[5]

Service with the Zouaves was so desirable that it was not unknown for non-commissioned officers of line regiments to renounce their stripes and to join the Zouaves as privates.[6] By the outbreak of the Crimean War in 1854, the three regiments of Zouaves comprised a body of nearly 10,000 experienced soldiers, well-trained and well-equipped.

* * *

Zouaves in Algiers, 1832. This contemporary French print depicts the first Zouaves to serve in the French army. The basic elements of the Zouave uniform are clearly distinguishable and remained relatively unchanged through the nineteenth century. The man on the right carries a guide flag stuck in the muzzle of his musket.

French Imperial Guard Zouave "sous-chef de musique," c. 1860. The Arab influence on Zouave dress in accentuated in the uniform worn by this principal musician, even to the point of his carrying a scimitar.

French Zouave, c. 1860. This woodcut originally appeared in a French newspaper, and probably illustrates the most popular conception of a Zouave soldier. In typical marching order, this Zouave carries tent poles, mess gear and an odd assortment of impedimentia. Note that he has decorated his canteen with his unit and a crescent moon and star.

CRIMEA AND ITALY

It was apparently during the Crimean War, however, that the Zouaves received widespread public notice outside France. In 1854, after France's declaration of war on Russia, two battalions per regiment of Zouaves were mobilized for the war. The remaining battalions of the regiments remained in Africa where the last of the Arab strongholds were being seized and the conquest of Algeria completed. The war battalions, of approximately 2,200 men from each regiment, took three months to organize; the six battalions reaching Constantinople in June of 1854.[7]

The Crimean War received wide coverage in the newspapers for it was the first major conflict since the Napoleonic Wars. In addition, this war was brought home as none before could have been because the development of popular journalism had created a vast reading audience who devoured especially the illustrated weeklies of the Victorian era. It might have seemed as though the Zouaves were created for the media. Their gaudy, oriental uniforms coupled with their roguish behavior and unquestioned bravery guaranteed that the Zouaves would gain the public's attention.

Interestingly, the Zouaves themselves had been eager to go to the Crimea to win "greater importance in the eyes of the world."[8] They wanted to prove that although they had been fighting guerilla warfare in Africa, they were capable of the "grander operations of a European war."[9] So great was the desire to go to the war in the East that many were bitter to be left behind. One *cantiniere** of the 2nd Regiment, who was left in depot because of her age and infirmities (she had served the regiment for twenty years), disguised herself as a soldier and attempted to slip aboard ship before it set sail.[10]

The Crimean War became especially noted for the hardships endured by the soldiers in that inhospitable country. The allied armies (French, English and Turkish) were racked first by cholera and dysentery, then by the weather and storms and finally by the breakdown of their supply systems. Unprepared for winter, the discomforts of the camps were immense. The battles were as equally demanding and from Alma to the final siege at Sebastopol the Zouaves were foremost among the brave.

One result of the Crimean War was the creation of a regiment of Zouaves within the French Imperial Guard. Also, because of this war three regiments of *Tirailleurs Algeriens* were formed from the single regiment which had existed since 1854. The *Tirailleurs,* more commonly known as Turcos, were also originally formed from various native soldiers found in Algeria. There were several independent organizations of these "sharpshooters" before their consolidation in 1841. Their growth had been fostered by the gradual replacement of native troops in the Zouave regiments with French men. The Turcos saw combat in most of the battles of the Crimean War, but never gained the popular acclaim of their European counterparts.

In 1859 Italian patriots in Sardinia, supported by the promises of Napoleon III of France, provoked a war with Austria. As the French Army sought to maintain the Piedmont and champion Italian independence, the Zouaves were once more in the thick of the fighting. Zouave units won many honors and their gallant conduct at such battles as Magenta and Solferino once more made the newspapers. In fact, so widespread was the knowledge of the French Zouaves that even in Tucson, Arizona the following filler was found in the daily paper without need of explanation:

> The ZOUAVES. Some of the Austrians seem to have been particularly struck at seeing Zouaves (sic) come into action with their pipes in their mouths. The German's love for a pipe is of the number of calm delights — a thing to be appreciated when "he beside his cottage door is sitting in the sun" — but a pipe in battle! Innocent German! Incomprehensible Zouave![11]

During the war in Italy "Harper's Weekly" ran illustrations of French Zouaves or Turcos in action in seven of the eight issues concerning the war. Clearly, the American public had ample opportunity to become familiar with the word Zouave long before the Civil War began. The Zouave uniform and fame was as well-known on this side of the Atlantic as in Europe, and it was only natural that there would be zouave imitators in the New World.

* * *

> * *Cantinieres and vivandieres were female sutlers employed by the French Army to sell wine, food and provisions within a regiment. Traditionally they were wives of soldiers of the regiment and wore quasi-military uniforms.*

French Zouave in the Crimea. Here the Zouave wears the hooded cloak used as an overcoat by Zouaves and Turcos. Interestingly, this carte de visite was made by an Albany, New York photographer.

Zouaves at the Battle of Alma, 20 September 1854. The Allied forces of France and Great Britain stormed strong Russian positions shortly after landing in the Crimea. It was the Crimean War which first thrust Zouaves into the public limelight, and heroic scenes such as this were frequently reproduced.

The storming of the Redan. During the Siege of Sebastopol during the Crimean War, French Zouaves led a charge on a part of the Russian fortifications known as the Redan. Breaking through the Russian lines, the Zouaves were ultimately driven back in hard fighting.

DISTRIBUTION OF MEDALS, BY THE EMPEROR OF THE FRENCH, TO THE ZOUAVES FROM THE CRIMEA.

The popular illustrated newspapers were filled with depictions of Zouaves. This scene of Napoleon III distributing medals to veteran Zouaves of the Crimea appeared in the **Illustrated London News.**

Group of French Zouaves from the Second Zouave Regiment with vivandiere, c. 1860. These European Zouaves pose while watching one of their officers accept a small refreshment from the vivandiere's keg.

THE ZOUAVE UNIFORM

Perhaps as significant to the creation of the Zouave legend as their prowess in battles, the uniform worn by the French Zouaves was a marked contrast to that of their comrades who wore traditional military uniforms. In 1830, when the first Zouave units were being formed, the European soldier was clothed in a tight, high-collared, tailed coat worn with pantaloons and a stiff military cap. His movements were further limited by the confining cross belts from which his accoutrements, usually cartridge box, bayonet and short sword, were hung.

In contrast, the original Zouaves wore loose and baggy trousers, a short, open jacket and a fez and turban for his headgear. This was in actuality the dress of local Turkish and African populace. Originally the dark blue jacket was trimmed with red on the edges only. The vest was also dark blue, with red pants and a blue sash. All garments were made of cotton cloth. The turban and fez were red.

By 1833, however, the jacket and vest were fully trimmed with red tape and the basic form of the Zouave uniform would thereafter be unchanged. Ultimately the uniform was made of woolen cloth of the same quality as the uniforms of the standard regiments. The red tape trim on the jacket formed an ornate design consisting of a loop leading into a trefoil or cloverleaf known as a *tombeau*. With the creation of three distinct regiments in 1852 the *tombeau's* loop was distinctively colored to identify the regiment — red for the 1st, white for the 2nd, and yellow for the 3rd. The cuffs of the jacket sleeves were open nearly to the elbow at the rear, but could be closed with hooks and eyes. The vest worn under the jacket was sleeveless and was buttoned at the side and top. It was also trimmed with red tape and had two shallow, open pockets at the front.

The distinctive Zouave trousers were made of a dull red *(garance)* wool. This garment took its name *(serouel)* and form from the loose Arab trousers worn in North Africa. Zouave trousers were not made with legs, but were instead basically just two large squares of cloth sewn together with openings for the legs. They had two pockets, trimmed with blue cord *(soutache)* in an ornate pattern around the pocket opening and as two parallel lines on either side of the pockets.

The trousers were placed into white canvas leggings which were in turn covered with leather greaves *(jambieres)*. Around their waist, the Zouaves wrapped blue woolen sashes which covered the tops of the trousers.

The Zouave's traditional headgear was a fez *(chechia)* with dark blue tassel. In full dress uniform the fez was wrapped with a turban. Originally, the turban was of red cloth, which was changed to green in 1852 and white by 1870.

The Zouaves of the Imperial Guard wore the same uniform, except that the jackets had red cuffs and were trimmed with yellow. The trousers of the Imperial Guard Zouaves had yellow cord decorations and the fez had a yellow tassel and white turban.

The *Tirailleurs Algerien's* uniforms were exactly like those of the Zouaves, except the jacket, vest and trousers were made of light blue wool. All trim on these uniforms was done with yellow tape or cord. Their fez was also red with blue tassel, but the turban was always white.

Both Zouaves and Turcos wore white cotton trousers in summer and for drill purposes. These trousers had no ornamentation. Such were the uniforms which inspired so many artists and illustrators and which would be imitated in countless variations in the United States. Indeed, while the French Zouave uniform remained fundamentally unchanged from the 1840's until the beginning of the Second World War, American Zouaves wore uniforms that ranged from almost exact copies of the original style to uniforms that were so modified as to be Zouave in name only.[12]

* * *

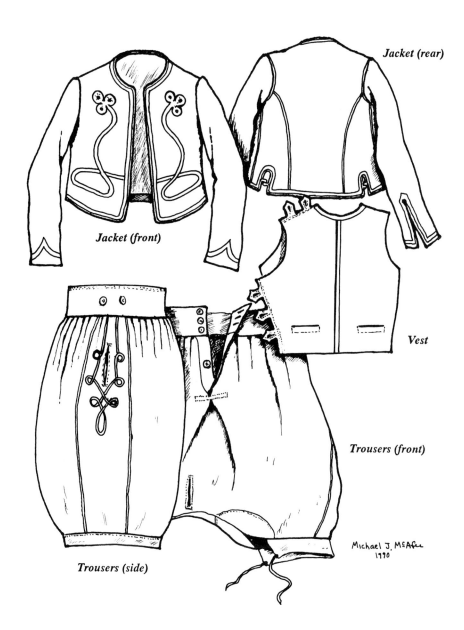

Components of the French Zouave uniform.

French Zouave, circa 1890. Although this carte de visite is from the late 19th century, this Zouave is uniformed much the same as his mid-century comrades. The patterns of jacket, vest and sash remained relatively unchanged until the First World War ended the colorful, traditional French uniforms.

The native soldiers who comprised the Tirailleurs Algerians or "Turcos" wore a distinctive light blue uniform with yellow trim. This non-commissioned officer has added extra trim on his vest, a very common deed among both Turcos and Zouaves.

ELMER E. ELLSWORTH AND THE AMERICAN ZOUAVE

Despite the successes of the Zouave in the Crimean War, it was not until 1859 that the first widely-publicized American Zouave unit was formed. This organization, The United States Zouave Cadets, was created from a moribund Chicago volunteer company by Elmer E. Ellsworth, a young idealist with a military persuasion. Ellsworth had become acquainted with one Charles A. DeVilliers, a former surgeon in the French Army in Algiers, who had served with a Zouave regiment during the Crimean War. One of Ellsworth's biographers credits this association as being "the turning point in Ellsworth's life" as it led him to popularize French Zouave uniforms and tactics in this country.[13]

Ellsworth, in his zeal, went so far as to impose the strictest of moral discipline upon his Zouave Cadets. No Zouave Cadet was allowed to drink, gamble, play billiards or act in any way "unbecoming to a gentleman".[14] Such restrictions would have been totally ignored by the true Zouaves of France! Ellsworth's men, a company of the 60th Regiment, Illinois State Militia, soon became the undisputed champions at local drill competitions. Their military exercises were based on the French Zouave drill, and the gymnastic antics of Ellsworth's Zouaves soon caught the public eye. Newspapers began carrying accounts of their feats, and especially, of the brilliant uniforms Ellsworth had designed for his unit. Actually, The Zouave Cadet had four uniforms. The first they adopted was a "full dress" uniform which, while of French style, was not at all a Zouave uniform. It consisted of a dark blue frock coat, blue-gray trousers and French forage cap. A second uniform, a "chasseur uniform" was created by wearing red trousers with the dress frock coat. They also had a "fatigue uniform" which was a scarlet jacket and pants worn with gaiters and a red cap.[15] The actual Zouave uniform of the men was worn for the first time in August of 1859. It was described by one of the Zouave Cadets later as follows:

> A bright red chasseur cap with gold braid; light blue shirt with moire antique facings; dark blue jacket with orange and red trimmings; brass bell buttons, placed as close together as possible; a red sash and loose red trousers; russet leather leggings, buttoned over the trousers, reaching from ankle halfway to knee; and white waistbelt.[16]

So confident was Ellsworth of the abilities of his company that in September of 1859 he issued a challenge to "any company of the Militia or regular Army of the United States or Canada" to meet in competition for a stand of Championship Colors.[17] When none accepted his challenge, he decided to seek out competition and a grand tour of Eastern cities was arranged by which he would exhibit the prowess of his Zouave Cadets.

On 2 July 1860 Ellsworth's excursion left Chicago with fifty picked men and the first drill was held at Adrian, Michigan on 4 July. From there the Zouave Cadets proceeded to Detroit, Cleveland, Niagara Falls, Rochester, Syracuse, Utica, Troy, Albany and New York City. The Zouaves reached New York City on 14 July and were met by a detachment of the 6th Regiment, New York State Militia. As the volunteer companies and regiments of the New York City area included some of the best trained and equipped units in the country, this was obviously the high point of the tour. On 17 July the Zouave Cadets visited Brooklyn where they were the guests of the 13th Regiment and gave drills at Fort Greene. When the visiting Zouaves left on the 20th, they left with tremendous plaudits and their uniforms and drill were pictured in the several illustrated weeklies published in New York which did even more to spread their fame throughout the entire country.

The Zouaves proceeded to Boston, West Point (where they performed for the Corps of Cadets and Lieutenant General Winfield Scott), Philadelphia, Baltimore, Washington, D.C., Pittsburgh, Cincinnati, St. Louis, and then returned to Illinois. When the Zouaves arrived in Chicago on the evening of 14 August 1860, it seemed as though the entire city was awaiting them. The grand tour of the Chicago Zouaves had made Ellsworth a popular hero, and it would also spawn dozens of other Zouave companies.[18] Some of these imitators would become noteworthy in their own right such as the Albany Zouave Cadets of New York and the Salem Zouaves of Massachusetts. However, most would soon be eclipsed by the stature of the volunteer Zouave regiments which would be raised within the next year because of the outbreak of the Civil War.

Ellsworth, meanwhile, left the Zouave Cadets and joined Abraham Lincoln's law office. With Lincoln's election, Ellsworth hoped to create a Militia Bureau within the Federal Government, which he, naturally, would head. Fate intervened, however, and Ellsworth, recently commissioned a second lieutenant in the Regular Army, resigned his commission and left Washington for New York City. There he would enlist a regiment of Zouaves, with himself as Colonel, from the men of the New York Fire Department. Ellsworth was not alone in such plans, as by 1861 there were many Zouave units competing for recruits.

* * *

The most reproduced portrait of Ellsworth shows him while on tour with his Zouave Cadets in 1860. It was photographed in Mathew Brady's New York studio.

Elmer E. Ellsworth, standing, sword in hand, right center, and his United States Zouave Cadets, 1860. The cadets here wear the company's "full dress," or non-Zouave uniform. (Photograph from the Kenneth Dunshee Collection.)

This 1860 lithograph sheet music cover depicts three of the U.S. Zouave Cadets uniforms. The figure on the far left is wearing the "full dress" of the company. Next is the Zouave dress. Ellsworth himself is third, in the full dress uniform. Finally, the figure on the far right wears the "chasseur" uniform. (West Point Museum Collections.)

Zouaves of the United States Zouave Cadets in New York City, July 1860. This woodcut from Frank Leslie's Illustrated Newspaper *has been frequently reproduced as "Civil War Zouaves." In actuality, the Zouave Cadets were disbanded before the war began. A group of former members did, however, organize the "Chicago Zouaves" and serve in the war.*

The Zouave Cadets' tour created considerable interest. This woodcut appeared in a New York City newspaper as part of a series depicting the drill of the Cadets.

Private John Langdon Ward, "Salem Zouaves," 1861. The "Salem Zouaves" were founded as the Salem Light Infantry in 1805. As a result of the election of Arthur F. Deveraux, a former business partner of Ellsworth, to the company as captain in 1860, the company renamed itself. Ward is seen here in the dark blue and red full Zouave uniform received while the company served in the 8th Regiment, Massachusetts Volunteer Militia, as Company I.

Albany Zouave Cadet, Louis C.B. Graveline, 1861. The Albany Zouave Cadets were formed in direct imitation of Ellsworth's touring Zouave Cadets. The company became Company A, 10th Regiment New York State Militia and later National Guard, State of New York.

Drummer, Albany Zouave Cadets, c. 1864. Only the letters "AZC" identify this musician as a member of a Zouave company. His cap is a regulation New York National Guard cap, and the triple breasted jacket with striping was common for musicians.

Colonel Robert B. Clark, 13th Regiment, New York State Militia. Although the 13th had only one Zouave company, again probably formed in response to the Zouave Cadet tour, Colonel Clark affects the dress of a Zouave.

This member of Company B, 13th Regiment New York State Militia, wears the Zouave uniform of his company. The other companies of the 13th Regiment wore gray jackets and trousers of the traditional style. (Photograph from the Frederick P. Todd Collection.)

Unidentified private, Boston Light Infantry, 1861. The Boston Light Infantry was one of the older independent companies in the Massachusetts Volunteer Militia, and had worn traditional uniforms for decades, including bearskin caps. However, just prior to the Civil War, and probably as part of the Zouave craze generated by Ellsworth, they adopted a dark blue Zouave uniform. The jacket, trousers and vest were trimmed in yellow-orange cord.

The United States Zouave Cadets were hosted by a number of militia units during their tour. Here a Zouave Cadet is flanked in Brooklyn by two members of the 13th Regiment, New York State Militia.

One of a series of photographs made by the New York City photographer, J. Gurney, this group shows Ellsworth (arms folded, left) with two officers of the Zouave Cadets (right) and three of the 6th Regiment, New York State Militia. The officer on the far left is Colonel Joseph C. Pinckney, and the tall officer behind the pillar is probably Lieutenant Colonel Samuel K. Zook.

ZOUAVES OF THE CIVIL WAR

It is obvious that Elmer Ellsworth and his United States Zouave Cadets spread the fame of the Zouave name throughout the United States. It is equally obvious that his tour inspired the creation of many Zouave companies wherever they went. However, it should be remembered that other Zouave companies existed before Ellsworth's grand tour and were not raised in imitation of his unit. In Pittsburgh, for example, the Pittsburgh Zouaves were among the companies which greeted Ellsworth's touring Zouave Cadets. In Philadelphia, the Philadelphia Zouave Corps, complete with uniformed *Vivandiere* was depicted in a colorful lithograph probably published in 1860, before Ellsworth's visit. Not only had the French Zouaves received popular acclaim in the press, but the official report on the armies of Europe, prepared by Captain George B. McClellan* as a result of the Crimean War, contained a glowing description of the Zouaves as well:

> The Zouaves are all French; they are selected from among the old campaigners for their fine physique and tried courage, and have certainly proved that they are what their appearance would indicate, — the most reckless, self-reliant, and complete infantry that Europe can produce.
> With his graceful dress, soldierly bearing, and vigilant attitude, the Zouave at an outpost is the beau-ideal of a soldier.[19]

Thus, the Zouave had found official praise even with the United States Army and, although it is difficult to gauge the effect of this report on the volunteer companies, it is obvious that Ellsworth was not the only American soldier familiar with Zouaves. Also, it should be remembered that wherever French immigrants were to be found there would also be volunteer companies with French uniforms. New York City, with a large French population, was not an exception. The "Gardes LaFayette" had existed as a French uniformed company for many years before it became the nucleus of the 55th Regiment, New York State Militia. Trained and uniformed as French Infantry, the 55th Regiment included all the components of a French line infantry unit, even to sappers wearing bearskin caps,** and, of course, a Zouave company.

It is not surprising, then, that New York would soon see the creation of a large number of volunteer Zouave regiments which would serve during the Civil War. Despite Ellsworth's eagerness to recruit the first regiment of the war, he was not able to do so, and on 23 April 1861, the first New York Zouave regiment was mustered into federal service. This regiment became the 9th New York Volunteer Infantry and was popularly known as "Hawkins' Zouaves."

The Hawkins' Zouaves had their origins in a pre-war military club formed in New York City on 23 July 1860, obviously as a result of the visit of Ellsworth and his Zouave Cadets. This group, evidently never a part of the New York militia system, called itself "The New York Zouaves" and was headed by Mr. Rush C. Hawkins, with Sergeant Louis Benzoni, a U.S. Regular soldier, as its drill master. Hawkins was the first man to reach Albany and offer to raise a regiment when the war broke in April of 1861. With the club as a nucleus, a regiment was quickly raised and on 23 April 1861, the first companies were sworn into federal service.[20]

Ellsworth, meanwhile, was busy recruiting from the New York City Fire Department. He was quoted as saying, "I want the New York Firemen, for there are no more effective men in the country, and none with whom I can do so much. They are sleeping on a volcano at Washington and I want men who can go into a fight now."[21] At the same time Colonel Abram Duryee, late of the 7th Regiment, New York State Militia, was organizing an "Advance Guard", which would soon become the 5th Regiment, New York Volunteer Infantry, or "Duryee's Zouaves." In New York City alone, in April and May of 1861, four complete regiments were organized and uniformed in the zouave style. These were the 5th New York (Duryee's Zouaves), the 9th New York (Hawkins' Zouaves), 10th New York (National Zouaves) and the 11th New York (Ellsworth's Fire Zouaves). These units do not include the 6th New York (Wilson's Zouaves) which did not receive Zouave uniforms when it enlisted, nor the many companies of Zouaves which were incorporated into non-Zouave regiments.

Other cities and states also saw the creation of Zouave units. Many were older companies from the volunteer militia system which responded to the first call for three months volunteers, such as the Salem Zouaves, which became Company I, 8th Regiment, Massachusetts Militia. Some, however, were new units, as for example the 11th Indiana Volunteer Infantry (Wallace's Zouaves). This regiment was organized in April at Indianapolis, Indiana, by Lewis Wallace (later the author of *Ben Hur*) for three months service, and was typical of many of the early midwestern regiments in that it reorganized after its original service and went on to serve for the duration of the war.

The Zouaves, or at least groups calling themselves Zouaves, seemed to be everywhere in 1861. One French language newspaper commented, *"Ils pleut des Zouaves,"* and rightfully so, for there probably seemed to be Zouaves everywhere one looked in 1861. Yet, the quality of the units, their uniforms, and equipment varied greatly. Duryee's Zouaves and Wallace's Zouaves were two regiments which proved to be capable, well-led and served with distinction from 1861 until 1865, going through several reorganizations. On the other hand, not all of these Zouave regiments even made it through the War. Ellsworth's Fire Zouaves, although raised with much promise, seemed to lose their sense of purpose after Ellsworth's death on 24 May 1861, at the hands of a pro-secessionist hotel keeper in Alexandria, Virginia. Despite the fact that the regiment performed as well as most others at the first battle of Bull Run in July of 1861, it was sent back to New York for regrouping and never again saw significant action. The 11th was mustered out on 2 June 1862.

An even more disastrous example of a failure was the 53rd New York Volunteer Infantry. In August of 1861, one Lionel Jobert D'Epineuil, recently arrived from France, was able to convince the War Department that he was a veteran of the French Army and so received a provisional colonelcy to raise a regiment of Zouaves. D'Epineuil expected to raise his regiment from the French population of New York City, but in this he was disappointed for most who were willing to enlist were already in service with other regiments such as the 55th New York State Militia. By November, when the first battalion left for Annapolis, only 130 French-born were on the rolls of the unit. The rest of the men were of various nationalities, but the top officers were of French extraction.

Almost immediately the regiment began falling apart. D'Epineuil quarreled with his officers. Discipline began to suffer and desertions and absences without leave soared. Detailed to accompany an expedition against North Carolina, the 53rd missed the main body of the expedition because of their transport running aground. In the confusion that followed they were sent back to Annapolis where eventually it was disclosed that D'Epineuil was a total fraud and had never served in the French Army. Other charges soon followed and D'Epineuil resigned. On 26 February 1862, slightly more than four months after the regiment was mustered into federal service, General George McClellan directed that the 53rd be disbanded, and on 21 March, 1862, the D'Epineuil Zouaves ceased to exist. The regiment never saw combat as a unit and had certainly the worst history of any American Zouave organization.[22]

Most Civil War Zouave Regiments, however, served with distinction. After the first generation of volunteer regiments were formed in April and May of 1861, a second generation was organized in wake of the defeat of Bull Run. In Pennsylvania, for example, there were four new Zouave regiments raised: the 23rd (Birney's), 72nd (Baxter's), 95th (Gosline's) and 114th (Collis) Volunteer Infantry Regiments. These became excellent regiments serving through the entire war with exemplary records. The 114th became one of the most photographed Zouave regiments as a result of its service as a Provost Guard detachment for the Army of the Potomac in 1864, making it readily available to the photographer Alexander Gardner. Gardner's many photographs clearly depict the life and uniforms of a Federal Zouave unit late in the war.

By 1864, obviously, the Zouave uniform could scarcely have been unfamiliar to anyone, North or South. In fact, it continued to be so popular that in 1863, because of the expiration of the original Duryee's Zouaves' time of service, steps were evidently taken to assure that there would still be a Zouave uniform in the "Regular Division" of the Fifth Corps. According to the historian of the 146th New York Volunteers, which had been organized in October of 1862, a regimental uniform of the Zouave pattern was issued for the first time in June of 1863. By January of 1864, three regiments of this division had received and wore thereafter, only Zouave uniforms. They were the 140th and 146th New York and the 155th Pennsylvania Volunteer Infantry Regiments.[23] By the end of the war in 1865, the Army of the Potomac alone contained at least seven regiments which were distinctly dressed and prided themselves in being Zouaves. In this elite group was, of course, the 5th New York Veteran Volunteer Infantry, the lineal descendant of the original Duryee Zouave regiment.

There were Zouaves present at every major Civil War battle, from First Bull Run to Appomattox. Undeniably, the Zouave uniforms of the war were inspired by Victorian romanticism, but the courage and sacrifices of the men who wore them were far from merely romantic. Although American Zouaves would never again see combat, the Zouaves and their uniforms lingered on. At first there were national guard units who retained the Zouave uniforms and continued to wear surplus Civil War uniforms. In New York City, Rush Hawkins continued to command a regiment (the First Regiment, New York National Guard) which wore the very uniforms which had been manufactured for the 9th New York Volunteers during the Civil War. Then, as the veterans grew too old even for militia service, they formed veterans' societies and continued to don the fez, jacket and baggy trousers of the Zouave.

In one form or another, the Zouave uniform continued to be worn in the United States well into the twentieth century. Drill teams and fraternal organizations wore variations of zouave dress through the 1950s, but by then their tie to actual military units had been long broken.

> * *George B. McClellan (USMA 1846), later Major General and Commander of the Union Army of the Potomac, 1861-1862.*

> ** *Sappers, or pioneers, were soldiers chosen for their size and strength to lead the regiment on the march, and equipped with axes and saws, to remove any obstacles.*

* * *

Zouave and officer of the 55th Regiment, New York State Militia, c. 1861. The 55th was a French-speaking regiment, recruited from the French population of New York City. When the war came its militia colonel was unequal to the task of organizing a full-size regiment, and after many months of inaction he was replaced by Philip Regis Denis De Trobriand. De Trobriand's volunteer regiment retained a Zouave company.

Private, New York Zouaves, c. 1861. This independent company, organized by Rush Hawkins, became the nucleus of the 9th New York Volunteer Infantry. This simplified Zouave style uniform evolved into what became the government pattern Zoauve uniform by 1863.

Colonel Rush Hawkins, 1861. Hawkins had served in the Mexican War, later became a lawyer, and still later a collector of rare books and imprints. He was breveted brigadier general for his wartime services. Here he wears the dark blue and gold uniform of an officer of the Hawkins' Zouaves, 9th New York Volunteer Infantry.

Unidentified Hawkins' Zouave, c. 1861-62. This Zouave wears the standard Hawkins' Zouave uniform of a dark blue jacket, vest and trousers trimmed in deep red. His weapon is a M1855 rifle musket.

Officers of the 5th New York Infantry at Fort Monroe, Virginia, 1861. Most of the regimental staff appears in this scene, including (left-right): Major J. Mansfield Davies, Lt. B. Ellis (assistant surgeon), seated; Lieutenant Colonel G.K. Warren (with telescope); Reverend Dr. Gordon Winslow (Chaplain), seated at table: Adjutant Joseph Hamblin; Colonel Abram Duryee; and Surgeon Rufus Gilbert.

Group of the 5th New York, Duryee's Zouaves, near Fort Monroe, 1861. There is nothing smart or even Zouave-like about this rumpled group of volunteers waiting for their pot to boil. The square cut and distinctive tombeaux of the first pattern Duryee Zouave jackets is apparent on the man looking at the camera, center.

Private Samuel H. Tucker was mustered into Company C, 5th New York Volunteer Infantry on 9 May 1861. He served two years in the regiment and mustered out on 14 May 1863. Here he wears the full uniform of a Duryee Zouave, lacking only a white turban.

Photographed at Fort Federal Hill in Baltimore, this unidentified private wears the early uniform of the 5th New York Volunteer Infantry. He holds a M1842 musket, and note the distinctive light blue edging to his red sash.

Captain Churchill J. Cambreleng served in the 5th New York Volunteer Infantry until discharged for disability on 23 July 1862. Here he wears a specially trimmed vest with his dark blue coat, red trousers and red cap, which is trimmed with gold lace. The cap also has an infantry horn insignia with the numeral "5" in the loop.

Although this Zouave has identified himself as a "DZ" for Duryee's Zouave and "5" for 5th New York, he could be a recruit for the Second Battalion which would become the 165th New York. His uniform is of the pattern to which the 5th New York had evolved by 1862. This recruit has the swagger of a true Zouave.

Gustav F. Linquist had originally enlisted as a private in the 5th New York, but was made a Second Lieutenant of the 165th New York in November of 1862. He was discharged in September of 1865 as a captain of the 165th. Here he wears an officer's version of the Zouave jacket and a fez.

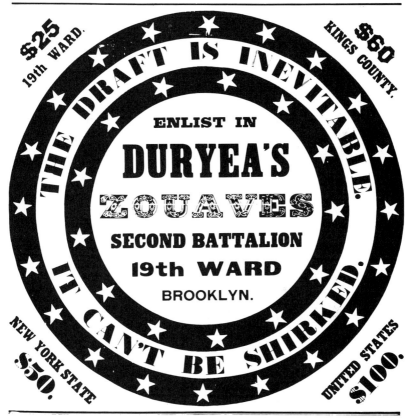

Recruiting Poster for the Second Battalion of the Duryee Zouaves. This unit would become the 165th New York, and be shipped to Louisiana to participate in the siege of Port Hudson. (Photograph from the Kenneth Dunshee Collection)

The Second Battalion, Duryee Zouaves, or 165th New York Volunteer Infantry, wore the Duryee Zouave uniform. This unidentified private wears a numeral "2" and the company letter "F" on the left edge of his Zouave jacket. Note that he wears the white turban with his fez.

Captain Thomas F. Meagher, seated, with members of Company K, 69th Regiment, New York State Militia, taken at Washington, D.C. in 1861. Meagher's company was the only one to wear Zouave dress in the 69th Regiment, and was disbanded when the regiment returned to New York City in August of 1861.

Colonel Robert ("Billy") Wilson, seated center, and members of the 6th New York Volunteer Infantry, 1861. Although called the "Wilson's Zouaves" when recruited, the original uniform of the regiment was of state-issued gray overshirts or blouses, gray trousers and brown or drab slouch hats. (National Archives photograph, #111-B-4388.)

The Salem Zouaves, 8th Regiment, Massachusetts Volunteer Militia, at City Hall in New York City, 1861. Detailed to sail the USS Constitution to the Navy Yard in Boston, the Zouaves stopped in New York for a record of their exploit.

This unidentified guide of Company A of the 23d Massachusetts Volunteer Infantry has placed the guidon's pole into the muzzle of his weapon. This uniform was inspired by that of the Salem Zouaves, and the company's captain, Ethan A.P. Brewster, had served in the Salem Zouaves earlier.

COLONEL LEWIS WALLACE AND STAFF.—ZOUAVE REGIMENT, ELEVENTH INDIANA VOLUNTEERS.

The 11th Indiana Volunteer Infantry, coloneled by Lewis Wallace, the central mounted figure in this woodcut, was initially uniformed in gray. The plain Zouave jackets and only slightly baggy trousers, both of gray cloth, were sparsely ornamented with red. Red caps, trimmed with blue, were also worn. The shirts under the jackets were of blue, and there was no proper Zouave vest worn.

Camp of the Wallace Zouaves, the 11th Indiana Volunteer Infantry, 1861. The men wear the original gray Zouave uniform of the Zouaves, with blue shirt and red kepi.

Private John L. Cook. Co. G, 11th Indiana Volunteer Infantry, c. 1861-62. Here Private Cook wears the new jacket of "black with a blue front that buttons up close," issued in December of 1861. His trousers are standard issue and of light blue. This uniform replaced the first issue of gray.

Ellsworth's First Fire Zouaves, the 11th New York Volunteer Infantry, wore gray uniforms until they began to wear out in June of 1861. At First Bull Run the regiment was uniformed in dark blue jackets and trousers, retaining their red fire shirts. Interestingly, the only Union regiment which seems to have worn red pants at Bull Run was the 14th New York State Militia. Contemporary descriptions of red-panted "Zouaves" would therefore have to mean the "Brooklyn Chasseurs," not the Fire Zouaves.

Death of Colonel Elmer E. Ellsworth, 24 May 1861. As Union forces entered the city of Alexandria, Ellsworth was determined to seize a Confederate flag which had been visible from the White House. After rushing into the Marshall House hotel, Ellsworth tore down the flag, but was killed as he left the roof by the proprietor James T. Jackson. Jackson was in turn killed by Zouave Francis E. Brownell.

The avenger of Ellsworth, Francis Brownell, left the 11th New York for a commission in the regular army. Here he wears the uniform from the fateful encounter with Ellsworth's assassin. His fireman's belt bears the name "Premier."

This unidentified private wears the Zouave dress of the 44th New York Volunteer Infantry-the "Ellsworth Avengers." As the regiment was also called the "People's Ellsworth Regiment," the letters "PER" are often seen placed on the cap tops of members. This dark blue and red uniform was obviously styled after the jackets of the Albany Zouave Cadets.

Union Zouaves marching down Pennsylvania Avenue. Artist unknown, after a Thomas Nast woodcut, 1861. Alexander McCook Craighead Collection, West Point Museum.

The Ninth New York Infantry, Hawkins Zouaves, leaving New York City, 6 June 1861. Watercolor by Herbert Knoetel. Alexander McCook Craighead Collection, West Point Museum.

The Eleventh New York Infantry, Ellsworth Fire Zouaves, in Alexandria, Virginia, 24 May 1861. Watercolor by Herbert Kroetel. Note that the uniform colors are inaccurate. Alexander McCook Craighead Collection, West Point Museum.

Zouaves of the French Imperial Guard, c. 1861. This contemporary French lithograph shows the detail of the French Zouave uniform as often copied by the American Zouave units.

Vivandiere of the Imperial Guard Zouaves, c. 1861. Note that the coloration of the uniform parallels that of the male Zouaves.

Vivandiere of the French Zouaves, c. 1861. The line Zouave uniforms were not so colorful as those of the Imperial Guard, and even the vivandiere lacks the gaudy features of her Imperial sister.

This 1861 patriotic envelope depicts a member of the Ellsworth Fire Zouaves departing from his family.

Felix Agnus served in both the 5th and 165th New York Infantry Regiments, and was made a Brevet Brigadier General in 1865. This tinted photograph clearly shows an officer's version of a Zouave uniform.

This period woodcut is one of the few contemporary illustrations of the ill-fated 53d New York, the D'Epineuil Zouaves. The regiment's performance never matched the elegance of its uniforms, unfortunately, and it was mustered out within months of its organization.

Captain Louis B. Hildebrand (center), First Sergeant William R. Peddle and "the captain's cook." The plain dark blue uniform of the 23d Pennsylvania Volunteer Infantry was trimmed in red cording, easily seen on Peddle's uniform.

The 23d Pennsylvania Volunteer Infantry, Birney's Zouaves, had a plain but attractive dark blue uniform with red cord trim on the jacket, vest and pants. This unidentified Zouave leans on a M1854 Lorenz rifle.

Hospital Steward of the 72d Regiment, Pennsylvania Volunteer Infantry-Baxter's Fire Zouaves. Here the dark blue jacket and cap, both trimmed with red, and light blue trousers with double red stripe are easily distinguished. Only the light blue vest is missing to complete the uniform.

The 72d Pennsylvania Volunteer Infantry, Baxter's Fire Zouaves, wore a very distinctive light blue vest as part of their full uniform. The unidentified sergeant shown here had his portrait tinted, the vest and trousers, light blue, and the jacket and vest trim, red.

DeWitt Clinton Baxter, organizer of the 72d Pennsylvania Zouaves, was a wood engraver and customs official in civilian life. He was made a brevet brigadier general for bravery at the Battles of Gettysburg and the Wilderness.

This unidentified enlisted man of the 95th Pennsylvania Volunteer Infantry, Gosline's Zouaves, wears the same blue jacket as worn by the 72d Pennsylvania. His vest and trousers, however, were dark blue, while the 72d wore light blue.

The "Zouaves d'Afrique" were organized by Charles H.T. Collis as an independent company in the late summer of 1861. It was to serve as bodyguard for Major General N.P. Banks. In 1862 Collis was promoted to colonel and expanded his "Zouaves d'Afrique" to a full regiment. Note the striping on the turban of this private.

After serious losses at the Battle of Gettysburg, the 114th Pennsylvania became headquarters guard for the Army of the Potomac. Here we see Company G, in August of 1864. Note the officer on the far left who wears a Zouave jacket.

One of the more unusual Zouave episodes of the Civil War was the use of mounted Zouaves in an 1861 skirmish in West Virginia. Piatt's Zouaves, the 34th Ohio Volunteer Infantry, wore blue jackets, not of Zouave style and light blue trousers, both trimmed in red. Their headgear included a tricorn hat, shown here being worn as slouch hats.

Private Lee Mathews, Company D, 76th Ohio Volunteer Infantry, wears a very distinctively-trimmed jacket. This style jacket was also worn by the 53d Ohio, and probably should not be considered a true Zouave uniform. However, its design was obviously influenced by the less spectacular trim on the jackets of the 33d New Jersey.

Drum Major John H. Naylor, 5th New York Veteran Infantry, c. 1864. Organized from veterans of the original 5th New York and recruits from several other regiments, the 5th Veterans served with distinction in the Virginia campaigns of 1864-65.

Unidentified corporal, 140th New York Volunteer Infantry, c. 1864. To commemorate the service of the original 5th New York in the Regular Division of the Fifth Corps, Zouave uniforms were presented to the several volunteer regiments in the division. The 140th wore blue jackets and trousers trimmed in red.

Unidentified corporal, 146th New York Volunteer Infantry, c. 1864-65. The Zouave uniforms received by this regiment, evidently in 1863, were close copies of the French Turco uniform, being of light blue with yellow trim.

Unidentified private, 155th Pennsylvania Volunteer Infantry, c. 1864. This wounded Zouave wears the blue and yellow Zouave uniform supplied to the 155th in 1864, and worn until the end of the war.

Published in the 16 December 1866 issue of **Harper's Weekly**, *this woodcut shows the First Regiment of Infantry, N.G.S.N.Y. on parade. The men wear the Hawkins' Zouave pattern uniform, and considered themselves the continuance of the Civil War regiment.*

Captain Almar Webster and Adjutant Mortimer L. MacKenzie, First Regiment, National Guard, State of New York, 1866. The reorganized New York National Guard included three veteran Zouave regiments in New York City. The First Regiment wore the uniforms and carried the battle honors of the Hawkins' Zouaves.

Drum Major Charles Blumenrather and drummer Henry M. Raggi, First Regiment, National Guard, State of New York. Many of the First Regiment's Zouave uniforms, such as worn by drummer Raggi, were surplus government Zouave uniforms left from the war, in this case, of the Hawkins' Zouave pattern.

Charge of the 9th New York Volunteer Infantry (Hawkins' Zouaves) at Roanoke Island, 8 February 1862. Given more press coverage than it was due, the Zouave charge was part of a general attack, and as is clearly seen in the woodcut originally published in Frank Leslie's Illustrated Newspaper, *other troops are entering the battery as the Zouaves charge.*

In the immediate post-war era Zouave companies were quite popular, and the many new Zouave units wore especially elaborate uniforms. Here the Springfield Zouaves of Springfield, Illinois display their post-war finery.

Peter Biegel, Color Corporal of Company C, 165th New York Volunteer Infantry, c. 1900. This proud Civil War veteran continued to parade with his regimental comrades into the twentieth century. Note that he carries a M1863 Remington "Zouave" rifle. The use of this handsome firearm by Zouave veterans after the war may have prompted its nickname as the "Zouave" rifle.

UNIFORMS OF THE CIVIL WAR ZOUAVE

Although the uniforms of the French Zouaves and Turcos were exotic and colorful, they were far surpassed by the imagination shown in designing uniforms for American Zouaves. When Ellsworth designed the Zouave uniform of his Zouave Cadets, his inspiration may have been from the French uniforms, but the end product lacked many of the traditional features of the Zouave uniform, including the fez, jacket tombeau and jambieres. The Zouave Cadets' uniform, however, was highly visible and it was copied widely by many pre-war Zouave organizations.

As a result, units such as the Salem Zouaves were clothed in uniforms even one step further removed from traditional Zouave styles, based as they were on interpretations of the originals. These quasi-zouave uniforms proliferated and were probably far more common than fully-rigged Zouaves such as the Philadelphia Zouave Corps. This same uncertainty of Zouave dress was common during the Civil War. Some regiments, such as Duryee's and D'Epineuil's clearly made an attempt to copy French Zouave dress. A few companies, such as the Zouave company of the 55th New York State Militia and Company "A" of the 74th New York Volunteers were also uniformed fully as Zouaves.

Most Civil War Zouave regiments, however, wore uniforms which were close to the original French uniforms, but differed in some slight details. The 9th New York and the 114th Pennsylvania were examples of this practice. The 9th wore fezzes, proper jackets and vests, but their trousers were dark blue and only slightly baggy. The 114th, on the other hand, wore red trousers, again, only slightly full, but with ornately trimmed jackets which had as a distinctive feature light blue cuffs. Neither regiment wore jambieres, but the 114th did wear a white turban with their fez. Both regiments presented an appearance which was quite close to that of the French Zouaves.

On the other hand, when Ellsworth organized his Fire Zouaves in New York City in 1861, he made no attempt to uniform them as French Zouaves. Instead he dressed them in a distinctive uniform that he had designed before the war began. This uniform was gray with blue and red trim, topped with a French Chasseur kepi of red with a blue band. No Zouave vest was worn, and in keeping with their name, the ex-firemen wore red fire shirts under their short gray jackets. Unfortunately, these original uniforms were made of shoddy material and they seem to have quite literally fallen apart in service.[24] They were replaced with more conventional Zouave uniforms of blue, but the red fire shirts were retained.

Thus, in 1861, the variety of dress among the so-called Zouave units was tremendous. Some were almost comical in their extremes, but many others showed taste and were quite attractive. It should also be remembered that not all units which called themselves Zouaves were uniformed as such. Many were Zouaves in name only. However, from this confused welter of styles there did emerge some distinctly American innovations in Zouave dress, and these should be noted.

The 11th Indiana (Wallace's Zouaves) was originally uniformed in a gray and red quasi-zouave uniform, which its colonel, Lewis Wallace, thought was more appropriate for Christians than the Moslem-inspired original. This uniform, however, was quickly replaced with a distinctive blue jacket. When the change was being contemplated Wallace wrote that the regiment felt "it was very desirable to keep up their identity as 'Zouaves'," and proposed to have new suits made for the regiment.[25] When they came they included standard Union Army skyblue trousers, but with the distinctive jacket. This garment was cut short, like a Zouave jacket, but rather than being open in front it had integral, distinctly-colored front pieces. These were meant to be buttoned, closing the jacket completely in front, while giving the illusion that the soldier was wearing a Zouave jacket over a buttoned vest. With this uniform the Wallace Zouaves continued to wear their original red caps, which were eventually replaced with blue ones. The Zouaves continued to wear their distinctive jackets through the remainder of the war, and they were evidently copied by other mid-western regiments after 1863.[26] Variations on this type of uniform were especially common in the Union Department of the Gulf, centered in Louisiana.

Interestingly, this same integral vest appeared in a few Zouave uniforms worn in the East as well. For example, the 76th Pennsylvania wore a traditional Zouave jacket with such a vest as did the 140th New York and 155th Pennsylvania. Although it is not possible at this time to accurately trace the origin of this style, it had been worn before the war. The 14th New York State Militia adopted a similar style in 1860 as a part of the chasseur uniform which they wore throughout their Civil War service as the 84th New York Volunteer Infantry. It is not known if this militia uniform had any part in the design of the vested jacket worn by Civil War volunteer units, but it could have been a precedent for them.

Another Americanized version of the Zouave jacket was worn by the 72nd and 95th Pennsylvania Volunteer Infantry Regiments. Both regiments were organized in Philadelphia in August of 1861, and both seem to have worn the same jacket. This garment was cut basically the same as a French Zouave jacket, except that its edges were all rounded. The cuffs were slit, but not buttoned or hooked as were French Zouave jackets, and the jackets had low standing collars. Along the edges of the jacket front, collar and cuffs was a double row of red tape. The front edges of the jacket were ornamented with ball buttons, as were the cuffs. In this aspect these jackets were quite similar to those of the original Zouave Cadets. While both regiments wore the same jacket, the rest of their uniforms differed. The 72nd wore light blue trousers and vests trimmed with red. The 95th wore dark blue vests with red cord trimming and small ball buttons and dark blue trousers. Both regiments wore leggings and dark blue forage caps. Although much of the original uniform was discarded as the war progressed, it is obvious from extant photographs that both regiments retained the distinctive Zouave jackets, wearing them with regulation clothing until the end of the war.

By 1863 the Zouave uniform, far from disappearing, enjoyed a continuing popularity. While this statement is contrary to the writings of many popular Civil War authors, it is well supported by photographic, illustrative and written evidence. It is also obvious that most soldiers accepted the Zouave uniform for what it was and did not find it at all comical or ludicrous. For example, when the 155th Pennsylvania received Zouave uniforms after having worn only the regulation blue since their enlistment, they were eager to make the switch:

> The exchange to the Zouave uniform from the plain infantry uniform was enjoyed immensely by the men...not only on account of their having earned the recognition, but also because of the great beauty of the uniform and the greater comfort and other advantages it possessed over the regulation uniform.[27]

Thus, like the French Zouaves, American soldiers found the Zouave uniform to be a source of pride and distinction.

Veteran Zouave regiments refused to relinquish their Zouave uniforms and did all they could to provide for their continued issuance. The Collis' Zouaves purchased enough material from France to last through the war in order to be assured of having their regimental uniforms.[28] Other regiments pressured the Quartermaster Department to provide replacements when their original uniforms wore out. By whatever means possible, Zouave uniforms were replenished throughout the war. In fact, one uniform refused to die even when its regiment was mustered out.

The 9th New York (Hawkins' Zouaves) was a "two year" regiment. In other words, when it was mustered in in 1861, its term of service was due to end in 1863. Some men, however, joined the regiment after its original recruitment and thus were obligated to serve after the regiment itself was mustered out. These veterans, as much Zouaves as the rest of the regiment, were transferred to another unit, only to learn that they were to have to give up the Zouave uniform of the 9th. Hearing this they literally mutinied and were allowed to retain their original uniforms until they wore out.

Later, when a veteran regiment to replace the 9th was recruited the original Hawkins' Zouave uniform was provided for it. As it happened though, the regiment was never filled and its men were transferred to the 17th New York

Veteran Infantry Regiment in October of 1863. However, the colonel of this regiment was so impressed by the uniform of the 9th that it was adopted by the 17th and worn for the remainder of the war.[29] In fact, the Hawkins' Zouave pattern was selected by the U.S. Army Quartermaster Department as a "standard pattern" zouave uniform. It was made in quantity and issued long after the 9th New York Regiment was mustered out of service. The 35th New Jersey and 164th New York were two regiments which were issued the Hawkins Zouave uniform late in the war.

Clearly, any assertion that the Zouave uniform was replaced with regulation clothing early in the war is mistaken. The Zouave regiments of the American Civil War were as proud of their distinctive dress as their French counterparts. It had induced many to join these regiments at the beginning of the war and remained a continuing source of pride throughout the war. At times these American Zouaves may have been ragged, for many refused to wear regulation clothing even when nearly naked, but their courage and conduct won for them a special place in the history of the American Civil War.

* * *

Lorenzo Clark, 74th New York Volunteer Infantry, c. 1861-62. Although Clark supposedly was not in the Zouave company of the 74th, he was photographed in its distinctive uniform. An unusual feature of this uniform was the placement of **tombeaux** *on both sides of the vest as well as the Zouave jacket.*

Sergeant of the 9th New York Volunteer Infantry, c. 1862. This photograph illustrates the standard Hawkins' Zouave pattern uniform of dark blue with dark red trim. Both black and white gaiters were worn with this Zouave uniform.

Although unidentified, this Zouave would seem to be a member of the 10th New York Volunteer Infantry-the National Zouaves. This regiment wore the letters "NZ" on its knapsacks and said they were the 10th New Zealand when asked. This private may be wearing a brown and red Zouave uniform supplied to the regiment early in its career.

Although more noted as an artist, James E. Taylor, Company B, 10th New York Volunteer Infantry, served as a Zouave for two years until May of 1863. Here Taylor wears the dark blue jacket, red vest and light blue trousers which constituted the final Zouave uniform of the 10th New York.

Captain Francis Fix of the 114th Pennsylvania Volunteer Infantry was wounded at the Battle of Gettysburg on 2 July 1863. Here he wears a red forage cap trimmed with gold, including the numbers "114" inside a wreath. Fix was discharged from service on 24 December 1863.

Private of the 114th Pennsylvania Volunteer Infantry, c. 1863. The distinctive light blue cuffs with red trefoil edging can be seen in this portrait. The unidentified private has dressed up in a white shirt and tie for his portrait.

Francis Brownell, 11th New York Volunteer Infantry, 1861. Brownell's often-reproduced portrait shows the red fireman's shirt and gray jacket and trousers which comprised the first uniform of Ellsworth's Fire Zouaves. Note that his red cap has a dark blue band and bears the company letter "A" and "1Z" for "First Zouaves."

Lieutenant Colonel Noah L. Farnham, 11th New York Volunteer Infantry, 1861. Farnham took command of the regiment upon Ellsworth's death, but was himself killed at the Battle of Bull Run in July of 1861. Fire Zouave officers also wore gray uniforms, trimmed with blue, red and gold.

Private, 11th Indiana Volunteer Infantry, "Wallace Zouaves," c. 1861-62. This, the second uniform of the 11th Indiana, was of a pattern which would become very popular for troops in the Department of the Gulf. Several regiments in the Department effected the Zouave-style jacket with integral false vest.

Private A.G. Garrett of the 34th Indiana Veteran Volunteer Infantry, c. 1864-65. Note that this integral false vest is of light blue. The diagonal veteran's stripe is visible on both sleeves.

Sergeant Henry Brown, Company B, 46th Indiana Veteran Volunteer Infantry, c. 1864. The uniform of the 46th included shoulder straps and simple border trim on the jacket.

The 100th Indiana Volunteer Infantry, in the jacket with integral vest. Note the "100" in oval on the right breast. (Original photograph now in the Daniel J. Miller Collection.)

Unidentified private of the 76th Pennsylvania Volunteer Infantry. This private wears the full Zouave uniform of the 76th. His braided cap has his company letter "C" applied to its chinstrap. Note the tie strings for the legs of his trousers dangling over the front of his jambieres *or leather greaves.*

*The uniform of the 76th Pennsylvania Volunteer Infantry-the Keystone Zouaves-featured a Zouave jacket with integral "false" vest of light gray. The **tombeaux** and tape trim were of a dark purple-red color, while the sash was red and the trousers a medium blue. Note that this sergeant also wears a veteran's stripe.*

Private J. Fred Tinker, Company K, 14th Regiment, NYSM, 1861. Tinker wears the distinctive blue and red quasi-chasseur uniform of the regiment. He was eventually commissioned as a lieutenant and mustered out with the regiment in 1864. The chasseur uniform of the 14th (84th New York Volunteer Infantry) is often confused with a Zouave uniform.

Sergeant Michael Lawn, 95th Pennsylvania Volunteer Infantry, 1864. Most Zouave regiments (as opposed to individual Zouave companies within a regiment) maintained their distinctive Zouave uniforms throughout the war, although often they were worn only for dress or other non-combatant duties. Here the Zouave jacket is worn with standard uniform parts.

This unidentified private of the 72d Pennsylvania has retained his Zouave jacket and a distinctive and non-regulation welt on his trousers. The McDowell-style forage cap on the chair clearly bears a white Second Corps badge, dating the photograph to the mid-1863 to 1864 time period.

Group of the 164th New York Volunteer Infantry, c. 1863-64. The 164th New York was one of several regiments issued Hawkins' Zouave uniforms in a attempt to standardize the variety of Zouave uniforms requested throughout the war.

Private Esli B. Dawson of the 33d New Jersey wears the all dark blue uniform with red trim of this regiment. Note the trefoils worked in the upper and lower corners of each side of the Zouave jacket. Note that the vest buttons are underlain with a strip of red cloth or tape. Noncommissioned officers of this regiment wore their chevrons in the inverted style of the U.S. Marine Corps, and both officers and men wore the numeral "33" on the front of their caps.

Major David B. Peloubet, 33d New Jersey Volunteer Infantry, wears the unusual officer's uniform of the regiment. The dark blue coats and caps of these officers were trimmed with red rather than gold lace. Their trousers, like those of their men, were dark blue.

Colonel John J. Cladek, 35th Regiment New Jersey Volunteer Infantry, 1863. The 35th was also issued Hawkins' Zouave uniforms, and Cladek's elaborate version was worn by the other officers as well.

This unidentified Zouave is believed to be a member of the "Phoenix Zouaves," an Irish-American quasi-military organization before the Civil War. The identification is based upon the similarity to a uniform worn by Thomas Meagher as an officer of the Phoenix Zouaves.

The uniform of the Burnside Zouaves of Providence, Rhode Island was quite distinctive. Here Sergeant J.B. Gardner holds his white kepi, and wears a light blue jacket and red trousers. The Burnside Zouaves served briefly during the war as a company of the 10th Rhode Island from May to September of 1862.

NOTES

1. Constant Lienhart and Rene Humbert, *Les Uniformes de l'Armee Francaise Depuis 1690 Jusqu'a Nos Jours* (Leipzig, M. Ruhl, 1900), III, p. 213.
2. Jean Joseph Cler, *Reminiscences of an Officer of Zouaves* (New York, D. Appleton & Co., 1860), p. 4.
3. Lienhart and Humbert, *Les Uniformes...*, p. 214.
4. Cler, *Reminiscences...*, pp. 10-11.
5. *Ibid.,* p. 5.
6. *Ibid.,* p. 11.
7. Paul Laurencin, *Nos Zouaves* (Paris, J. Rothschild, 1888), pp. 72-73.
8. Cler, *Reminiscences...*, p. 111.
9. *Ibid.,* p. 111.
10. *Ibid.,* p. 113.
11. Donald B. Sayner, Robert P. Hole and Margaret S. Brett-Harte, *Arizona's First Newspaper,* "The Weekly Arizonian" (Tucson, University of Arizona, 1977), n.p.
12. Many sources, including actual uniforms and original photographs, drawings and paintings were consulted for this chapter. Two recent and excellent articles have appeared on the uniforms of the zouaves. They are: Francois Calame, "Les Zouaves En Afrique, 1880-1914," *Gazette des Uniformes,* No. 30 (March-April 1976), pp. 5-14; J.L. Martel, "Les Zouaves," *Campaigns,* II, No. 8 (January-February 1977), p. 32.
13. Charles A. Ingraham, *Elmer E. Ellsworth and the Zouaves of '61* (Chicago, University of Chicago Press, 1925), p. 7.
14. Ingraham, *Elmer E. Ellsworth...*, p. 26.
15. Frederick P. Todd and H. Charles McBarron, "United States Zouave Cadets, 1859-1860," *Military Collector and Historian,* III, 3 (Fall 1951), pp. 71-72.
16. Ingraham, *Elmer E. Ellsworth...*, p. 32.
17. *Ibid.,* p. 60.
18. *Ibid.,* pp. 68-79.
19. George B. McClellan, *The Armies of Europe* (Philadelphia, J.B. Lippincott & Co., 1861), p. 61.

20. Matthew J. Graham, *The Ninth Regiment New York Volunteers* (New York, 1900), pp. 32-54.
21. Ingraham, *Elmer E. Ellsworth...*, p. 127.
22. Gerald E. Wheeler, "D'Epineuil's Zouaves," *Civil War History,* II, 4 (December, 1956), p. 93:100.
23. Harry T. Grube and Michael McAfee, "140th New York Volunteer Infantry, 1864-1865," *Military Collector & Historian,* XXII, 2, pp. 55-56; same authors, "146th New York Volunteer Infantry, 1863-1865," *Military Collector & Historian,* XXII, 2, p. 56; H. Charles McBarron, Jr. and Frederick P. Todd, "155th Pennsylvania Volunteer Infantry Regiment, 1864-1865," *Military Collector & Historian,* I, 3 (August 1949), p. 3-4.
24. *New York Daily News,* 2 July 1861, p. 8: *New York Tribune,* 21 August 1861, p. 8.
25. H. Charles McBarron, Jr. and Frederick P. Todd, "11th Indian Volunteers (Wallace Zouaves), 1861," *Military Collector & Historian,* III, 4 (December 1951) pp. 84-86.
26. Frederick P. Todd, *et al, American Military Equipage, 1851-1872* (Providence, The Company of Military Historians, 1974), pp. 53-55.
27. The 155th Regimental Association, *Under the Maltese Cross, Antietam to Appomattox* (Pittsburgh, 1910), p. 224.
28. Frank Rauscher, *Music on the March, 1862-'65, with the Army of the Potomac* (Philadelphia, 1892), p. 13.
29. Graham, *The Ninth Regiment,* pp. 450-452.

SELECTED BIBLIOGRAPHY

I. The French Zouaves

    Aumale, Henri Eugene. *Les Zouaves et Les Chasseurs a Pied.* Paris: Michael Levy, Freres, 1855.
    Cler, Jean Joseph. *Reminiscences of an Officer of Zouaves.* New York: D. Appleton & Co., 1860.
    DeChesnel, M.A. *Dictionaire des Armes de Terre et de Mer.* Paris: Alexander Labritte, c. 1863.
    Laurencin, Paul. *Nos Zouaves.* Paris: J. Rothschild, 1888.
    Lienhart, Constance and Rene Humbert. *Les Uniformes de L'Armee Francaise Depuis 1690 Jusqu'a Nos Jour.* Leipzig: M. Ruhl, 1900.
    McClellan, George B. *The Armies of Europe: Comprising Descriptions in Detail of the Military Systems of England, France, Russia, Prussia, Austria and Sardinia,...* Philadelphia: J.B. Lippincott & Co., 1861.
    Thorburn, W.A. *French Army Regiments & Uniforms from the Revolution to 1870.* New York: Hippocrene Books, Inc. 1976.

II. The American Zouaves

    Cowtan, Charles W. *Services of the Tenth New York Volunteers.* New York: Charles H. Ludwig, 1882.
    Davenport, Alfred. *Camp and Field Life of the Fifth New York Infantry (Duryee Zouaves).* New York: Dick and Fitzgerald, 1879.
    Graham, Matthew J. *The Ninth Regiment New York Volunteers (Hawkins' Zouaves).* New York: 1900.
    Ingraham, Charles A. *Elmer E. Ellsworth and the Zouaves of '61.* Chicago: University of Chicago Press, 1925.
    Johnson, Charles F. *The Long Roll: Being a Journal of the Civil War (Hawkins' Zouaves).* East Aurora, New York: 1911.
    Manning, James H. *Albany Zouave Cadets: Fifty Years Young.* Albany: 1910.
    The 155th Regimental Association. *Under the Maltese Cross (155th Pennsylvania Regiment).* Pittsburgh: 1900.
    Rauscher, Frank. *Music on the March, 1862-'65, with the Army of the Potomac* (114th Pennsylvania Regiment). Philadelphia: 1892.

INDEX

"Advance Guard," 40
Agnus, Felix, 68
Albany Zouave Cadets, 26, 31, 33, 64

Banks, N.P., 76
Baxter, DeWitt Clinton, 74
Baxter's Fire Zouaves, 41, 72, 73
Benzoni, Louis, 40
Biegel, Peter, 89
Birney's Zouaves, 41, 71
Blumenrather, Charles, 85
Boston Light Infantry, 36
Brewster, Ethan A.P., 57
"Brooklyn Chasseurs," 61
Brown, Henry, 104
Brownell, Francis E., 62, 63, 100
Burnside Zouaves, 116

Cambreleng, Churchill J., 50
Cantiniere, 14
"Chicago Zouaves," 26, 30
Cladek, John J., 114
Clark, Lorenzo, 94
Clark, Robert B., 34
Collis, Charles H.T., 76
Collis' Zouaves, 41, 92
Cook, John L., 60
Crimean War, 10, 14-15, 17, 39

Davies, J. Mansfield, 47
Dawson, Esli B., 112
D'Epineuil, Lionel Jobert, 41, 69, 90
De Trobriand, Philip Regis Denis, 43
Deveraux, Arthur F., 32
DeVilliers, Charles A., 25
Duryee, Abram, 40, 47
Duryee's Zouaves, 40, 41, 42, 47, 48, 51, 53, 54, 90

Ellis, B., 47
"Ellsworth Avengers," 64

Ellsworth, Elmer E., 25-29, 38, 39, 40, 41, 62, 63, 90
Ellsworth's Fire Zouaves, 40, 41, 61, 66, 68, 90, 100

Farnham, Noah L., 101
Fix, Francis, 98
French Army, 8
French Imperial Guard, 12, 14, 66, 67

"Gardes LaFayette," 39
Gardner, Alexander, 41
Gardner, J.B., 116
Garrett, A.G., 103
Gilbert, Rufus, 47
Gosline's Zouaves, 41, 75
Graveline, Louis C.B., 31

Hamblin, Joseph, 47
Hawkins, Rush C., 40, 42, 44, 45
Hawkins' Zouaves, 40, 46, 65, 83, 84, 86-87, 92, 93
Hildebrand, Louis B., 70

Illinois State Militia, 60th Regiment, 25
Indiana Veteran Infantry, 34th Regiment, 103; 46th Regiment, 104
Indiana Volunteer Infantry, 11th Regiment, 40, 58, 59, 60, 91, 102; 100th Regiment, 105

Jackson, James T., 62

Keystone Zouaves, 107

Lawn, Michael, 105
Lincoln, Abraham, 26
Linquist, Gustav F., 52

MacKenzie, Mortimer L., 84

Massachusetts Volunteer Infantry, 23rd Regiment, 57
Massachusetts Volunteer Militia, 8th Regiment, 32, 40, 56
Mathews, Lee, 78
McClellan, George B., 7, 39, 41
Meagher, Thomas F., 55, 115

National Zouaves, 40, 96
Naylor, John H., 79
New Jersey Volunteer Infantry, 33rd Regiment, 78, 112, 113; 35th Regiment, 93, 114
New York City Fire Department, 26, 40
New York National Guard, First Regiment, 42, 83, 84, 85
New York State Militia, 6th Regiment, 26, 38; 7th Regiment, 40; 10th Regiment, 31; 13th Regiment, 26, 34, 35, 37; 14th Regiment, 61, 91, 108; 55th Regiment, 39, 41, 43, 90; 69th Regiment, 55
New York Veteran Infantry, 5th Regiment, 42, 79; 17th Regiment, 92-93
New York Volunteer Infantry, 5th Regiment, 40, 47, 48, 49, 50, 51, 52, 68, 79, 80; 6th Regiment, 40; 9th Regiment, 40, 42, 44, 45, 65, 86-87, 90, 92, 93, 95; 10th Regiment, 40, 96, 97; 11th Regiment, 40, 41, 61, 63, 66, 100, 101; 44th Regiment, 64; 53rd Regiment, 41, 69; 74th Regiment, 90, 94; 84th Regiment, 91, 108; 140th Regiment, 42, 80, 91; 146th Regiment, 42, 81; 164th Regiment, 93, 111; 165th Regiment, 51, 52, 53, 54, 68, 89
"New York Zouaves," 40
North Africa, 9, 10

Ohio Volunteer Infantry, 34th Regiment, 77; 53rd Regiment, 78; 76th Regiment, 78

Peddle, William R., 70
Peloubet, David B., 113
Pennsylvania Volunteer Infantry, 23rd Regiment, 41, 70, 71; 72nd Regiment, 41, 72, 73, 74, 75, 91, 92, 110; 76th Regiment, 91, 106, 107; 95th Regiment, 41, 75, 91, 92, 109; 114th Regiment, 41, 77, 90, 98, 99; 155th Regiment, 42, 82, 91, 92
"People's Ellsworth Regiment," 64
Philadelphia Zouaves, 39, 90
"Phoenix Zouaves," 115
Piatt's Zouaves, 77
Pinckney, Joseph C., 38
Pittsburgh Zouaves, 39

Raggi, Henry M., 85
Rhode Island Volunteer Infantry, 10th Regiment, 116

Salem Zouaves, 26, 32, 40, 56, 57, 90
Springfield (Ill.) Zouaves, 88

Taylor, James E., 97
Tinker, J. Fred, 108
Tucker, Samuel H., 48
Turcos, 14-15, 24, 90

Uniform, parts, 20-22
United States Zouave Cadets, 25-26, 29, 37
USS Constitution, 56

Vivandiere, 19, 39, 67

Wallace, Lewis, 40, 91
Wallace's Zouaves, 40, 59, 91, 102
Ward, John Langdon, 32
Warren, G.K., 47
Webster, Almar, 84

West Point Museum, 5
Wilson, Robert ("Billy"), 56
Wilson's Zouaves, 40, 56
Winslow, Rev. Dr. Gordon, 47

Zook, Samuel K., 38
Zouave Regiment, First, 9, 20; Second, 9, 19, 20; Third, 9, 20
"Zouaves d'Afrique," 76

THOMAS PUBLICATIONS publishes books about the American Colonial era, the Revolutionary War, the Civil War, and other important topics. For a complete list of titles, please write to:

>THOMAS PUBLICATIONS
>P. O. Box 3031
>Gettysburg, PA 17325